PENGUIN BOOKS

HOW TO FIND LOST OBJECTS

Professor Solomon has worked as a bookstore clerk, substitute teacher, stage magician, and writer/actor in children's television. He is currently on the staff of a public high school. Among his duties is the maintenance of the lost-and-found.

How to Find Lost Objects

Professor Solomon

Penguin Books

PENGUIN BOOKS
Published by the Penguin Group
Penguin Books USA Inc., 375 Hudson Street,
New York, New York 10014, U.S.A.
Penguin Books Ltd, 27 Wrights Lane, London W8 5TZ, England
Penguin Books Australia Ltd, Ringwood, Victoria, Australia
Penguin Books Canada Ltd, 10 Alcorn Avenue,
Toronto, Ontario, Canada M4V 3B2
Penguin Books (N.Z.) Ltd, 182–190 Wairau Road,
Auckland 10, New Zealand

Penguin Books Ltd, Registered Offices:
Harmondsworth, Middlesex, England

First published in the United States of America by Top Hat Press 1993
Published in Penguin Books 1995

1 3 5 7 9 10 8 6 4 2

DRAWINGS BY STEVE SOLOMON
Photographs by Brad Fowler and Leonard Solomon

The author thanks Larry Callahan and
Elizabeth Minter for their assistance.

LIBRARY OF CONGRESS CATALOGING IN PUBLICATION DATA
Solomon, Professor
How to find lost objects/by Professor Solomon
p. cm.
Includes bibliographical references and index.
ISBN 0 14 02.4212 0
1. Lost articles—Humor. I. Title.
PN6231.L59S65 1995
818′ .5402—dc20 94–23416

Printed in the United States of America
Set in Adobe Garamond

Contents

1.
A Method That Works

2.
The Principles

3.
The Way to Search

4.
The Art of Finding

5.
This and That

How to Find
Lost Objects

1.
A Method
That Works

This Book's for You

You've lost your car keys, and are about to lose your mind.

You've looked everywhere—have torn your house apart—but can't find those keys.

Your day has ground to a halt. Your life is on hold. A glazed look has come into your eye. You're going nuts!

All because of a missing set of keys.

You begin another search. Like a wild man, you rummage through room after room. Half an hour later, they still haven't turned up. You throw yourself on the sofa and groan: "This is ridiculous!"

Finally, you check your pocket. For the keys? No, for the bus fare you're going to need to get to work. It's come to that.

Talk about feeling foolish.

Meanwhile, your neighbor has mislaid his checkbook.

Less than a minute later, he has found it, and is coolly walking out his front door.

How did he do it? How did he avoid the frustration—the inconvenience—the loss of time—so often caused by misplaced objects?

Let's ask him.

3

"Sir, how did you find that elusive checkbook?"

"Why, simple," he replies with a modest smile. "By applying the Twelve Principles."

"The Twelve Principles?"

"That's right. As outlined in How to Find Lost Objects by Professor Solomon."

And he continues on his way—while you are about to resume the frantic hunt for your keys.

But...maybe it's time that you, too, checked out those Twelve Principles.

Maybe you're ready, after all these years, to become a Finder, not a Loser.

If you think you might be—if you're seriously interested in *locating what you lose*—this book's for you.

The Facts

Young and old, rich and poor, city folks and farmers—we're all constantly losing things.

It's an age-old problem—as old as the pyramids. And one that's not about to go away.

Every day millions of objects are misplaced in the United States. Among them are wallets, rings, keys, scissors, sweaters, notebooks, eyeglasses, theater tickets, important documents—you name it. (A circus elephant is said to have been lost recently in Florida!) Many of these objects are never recovered —possibly a billion dollars' worth annually. (Their sentimental value, of course, is incalculable.) Even more disturbing is the time spent looking for such objects. The average person could spend up to *two months* of his life searching—often fruitlessly—for things he has lost.

Then there's the "nuisance factor" associated with missing objects. The cars that can't be started. The books that can't be read. The business that can't be conducted. Millions of Americans experience such frustrations daily. It is something that touches each of our lives, and that can make a nightmare of an ordinary day—that can drive us to distraction!

But the incredible fact is this:

Each and every one of those objects—the tickets, the eyeglasses, the elephant—could have been found. Easily. Within minutes.

Yes, lost objects can be found.

How is it done?

By following my method.

Interested?

Read on.

Getting Started

My method is unique, amazing, and easy to learn.

It is based on what I call the Twelve Principles—a set of precepts designed to lead you *directly* to any lost object. Like a bloodhound!

I discovered these principles after years of bitter experience. For I, too, was once a Loser and a Weeper. I, too, was constantly being mocked by misplaced keys, books, manuscripts, pajama tops. My cap would vanish. My pen would hide from me. The list was endless.

But then I realized that lost objects *can* be found. If one conducts the search systematically and is mindful of a few basic ideas.

It wasn't long before I was finding my things with an ease that seemed miraculous. Yet no psychic powers, expensive equipment, or special skills were involved. Simply a *method*. I also began to help friends find their lost items. Astounded at the results, they urged me to write this book.

You'll be astounded, too, as missing objects virtually *line up* to be found!

I recommend that you start by reading the book through from beginning to end. Introduce yourself to the Principles. Follow Betsy as she searches for her keys—the wrong way and the right way. Get a feel for my tips and techniques. And mark any sections that seem particularly relevant to your own misplacement profile.

Then, the next time you lose something, open this book and make the Twelve Principles work for you.

I can almost guarantee they will.

Are you ready?

Let's learn how to find lost objects.

On to the Principles.

2.
The
Principles

The Twelve Principles

My method is based on the Twelve Principles—a set of *fundamental guidelines* for finding lost objects.

The Twelve Principles are:

1. Don't Look for It
2. It's Not Lost—*You* Are
3. Remember the Three C's
4. It's Where It's Supposed to Be
5. Domestic Drift
6. You're Looking Right at It
7. The Camouflage Effect
8. Think Back
9. Look Once, Look Well
10. The Eureka Zone
11. Tail Thyself
12. It Wasn't You

These Principles are the core of my method. So get acquainted with them. Learn them. Master them.

Then, whenever something can't be found, simply *apply the Principles*.

So . . . let's get right into them.

PRINCIPLE ONE

Don't Look for It

Something's lost, and your first thought—your basic instinct—is to look for it. You're ready to start rummaging about. To hunt for it in a random, and increasingly frenetic, fashion. To ransack your own house.

This is the most common mistake people make. And it can doom their search from the start.

I know you're eager to find that lost item. But not yet. Don't look for it yet.

Wait until you have some idea *where* to look.

PRINCIPLE TWO

It's Not Lost—*You* Are

Have you ever stopped to think that maybe it's *you* that are lost—not those keys or that umbrella?

Because a fundamental truth is this:

There are no missing objects. Only unsystematic searchers.

Accept that—copy it down and tape it to your mirror—and you'll soon be finding things with ease.

PRINCIPLE THREE

Remember the Three C's

To find a lost object, you must be in the proper frame of mind. And that means paying attention to the Three C's.

They are:

COMFORT

Start by making yourself comfortable in an arm-chair or sofa. Have a cup of tea, perhaps, or stick of gum, or pipeful of tobacco.

CALMNESS

Next, empty your mind of any unsettling thoughts. Pretend that the sea is lapping at your feet. Or that you're sitting in a garden full of birds and flowers.

CONFIDENCE

Finally, tell yourself you *will* locate that missing object. (To enhance your confidence, you might want to don a thinking cap. See page 74 for instructions on how to make one.)

Now you're ready. To begin a *systematic* search.

PRINCIPLE FOUR

It's Where It's Supposed to Be

Believe it or not, things are often right where they're supposed to be.

Is there a place where your missing object is normally kept? A particular rack, or shelf, or drawer? If so, look there first. You may actually have hung up your coat last night. Or put the dictionary back on the shelf. Or returned the tape measure to the tool drawer.

Even if you didn't, someone may have done it for you.

PRINCIPLE FIVE

Domestic Drift

Many objects do have a designated or customary place where they are kept. But the reality is that they aren't always returned there. Instead, they are left *wherever last used.*

Such objects have undergone Domestic Drift. They could be anywhere in the house or out in the yard.

Relax. Get comfortable. Pour yourself a cup of coffee.

Now try to remember. Where were you last using that pliers, or tape measure, or fountain pen? Where did you last *have* it?

Because that's precisely where it still may be.

PRINCIPLE SIX

You're Looking Right at It

All right. You checked where it's supposed to be, where it was last used, or where it might have been casually tossed. And it wasn't there.

Or . . . was it?

It is possible to look *directly* at a missing object and not see it. This is due to the agitated state of mind that often accompanies a misplacement. Go back and look again. It may be staring you in the face.

Occasionally, our distress is such that not only do we overlook an object—we forget what we're looking for! To avoid this, repeatedly murmur the name of the object. ("Potholder, potholder, potholder.")

But why the agitation? Have we forgotten the second C? Return to your armchair and get calm.

PRINCIPLE SEVEN

The Camouflage Effect

Don't be fooled. Your object may be right where you thought it was—but it has become *hidden from view*. Be sure to check under anything that could be *covering* your object, having inadvertently been placed on top of it.

I call this the Camouflage Effect. Among the most common offenders are newspapers and sombreros.

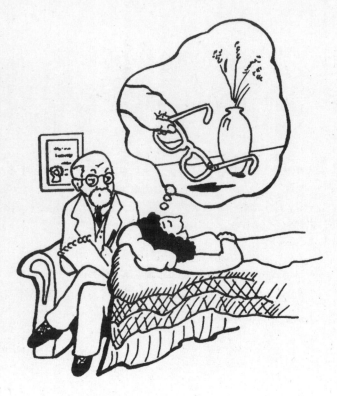

PRINCIPLE EIGHT

Think Back

You were there at the scene of the misplacement.

You were there when the object was put down—was left in an obscure location—was consigned to oblivion.

You were there—because you did it!

So you must have a memory—however faint—of where this happened.

Are you prepared to *think back* and retrieve that memory?

If so, you may soon be crying out "Of course!" and making a beeline to that forgotten place.

PRINCIPLE NINE

Look Once, Look Well

Don't go around in circles. Once you've checked a site, don't go back and check again. No matter how promising a site—if the object wasn't there the first time, it won't be there the second.

Assuming, of course, that your first check was *thorough*.

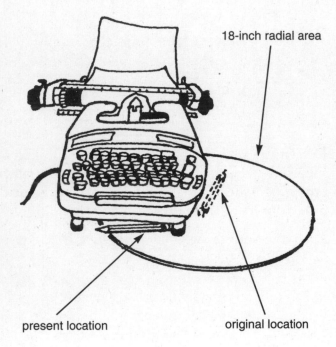

18-inch radial area

present location

original location

The Eureka Zone

The majority of lost objects are right where you figure—once you take a moment to stop and figure.

Others, however, are in the *immediate vicinity* of that place. They have undergone a displacement—a shift in location that, although minor, has served to render them invisible.

Some examples:

A pencil has rolled beneath a typewriter.

A tool has been shoved to the rear of a drawer.

A book on a shelf has gotten lodged behind other books.

A folder has been misfiled, several folders away from where it belongs.

Objects are apt to wander. I have found, though, that they tend to travel no more than *eighteen inches* from their original location. To the circle described by this eighteen-inch radius I have given a name. I call it the Eureka Zone.

With the aid of a ruler (or a Eureka-Stik—see page 76), determine the Eureka Zone of your lost object. Then explore it. Meticulously.

Tail Thyself

If you still haven't found your object, it may be time to Recreate the Crime.

Remove your thinking cap and don your detective's cap. For you are about to *follow your own trail.*

Let's create a typical scenario. You come home from work and find a letter in the mail. Some time later you're ready to read it…but it's missing. You're perturbed and perplexed. Where's that letter?

Okay, start at the door and retrace your steps since returning home. Where in the house did you go? To what specific locations? Stop at each of them and look for the letter.

Hmm, a coat thrown across a chair. You were here. (Check under the coat and in its pockets.)

A depression in the sofa. You were here.

On the kitchen counter, a glass. You were here.

On the table by the armchair, candy wrappers and a novel. You were here.

And marking your place in the novel—aha! That missing letter.

Good work, gumshoe.

PRINCIPLE TWELVE

It Wasn't You

When all else has failed, explore the possibility that your object hasn't been misplaced. Rather, it's been *misappropriated.*

Perhaps someone you know has borrowed your umbrella. Or eaten your doughnut. Or taken your magazine into another room.

Approach that person and inquire if such might not be the case. ("Have you by any chance seen my . . . ?" is a tactful way to phrase this.)

Quiz

Let's see if you have mastered the Principles. Check true or false to each of the following statements:

1. If you misplace something, search your entire house for it. Do so in a frenzied, unsystematic fashion. Do *not* use the Twelve Principles.

☐ true   ☐ false

2. Never check under a sombrero for a missing object.

☐ true   ☐ false

3. The Three C's are Confusion, Consternation, and Discomfort.

☐ true   ☐ false

4. The Eureka Zone is a mountainous area of the Yukon, in which gold was discovered in 1848.

☐ true   ☐ false

5. Poltergeists, gremlins, and other supernatural beings are responsible for the majority of lost objects.

☐ true   ☐ false

6. Domestic Drift is a term used by bureaucrats to refer to houses that float off during a flood.

☐ true   ☐ false

7. A misplaced elephant cannot be found.

        □ true   □ false

8. There are twelve months in the year, twelve members of a jury, twelve signs of the zodiac, and Nine Principles for finding lost objects.

        □ true   □ false

When you have completed the quiz, turn the page.

If you answered false to each of the eight questions, congratulations! You have mastered the Twelve Principles. Welcome to the ranks of those who locate what they lose.

One More Principle

The following principle is a special one.

I call it the THIRTEENTH PRINCIPLE. And I have kept it apart from the others to underscore its use in a certain dire situation only.

The situation is this: *You've applied each of the Twelve Principles, and still haven't found your object.*

That should rarely happen. But when it does, you have a recourse—the THIRTEENTH PRINCIPLE.

Okay, turn the page and take a look.

The Thirteenth Principle

Qué Será, Será

Have you been applying the Principles? If so, you should have found your object by now.

But occasionally, Fate chooses to separate us from one of our possessions. When that seems to be the case, it's time to *call off the search.*

Your missing object may eventually turn up. Until then, accept that you are being offered a lesson: in patience . . . or humility . . . or nonattachment to the things of this world.

And if not, so what? Lost keys, books, eyeglasses—even elephants!—can be replaced. Such losses are inconvenient and vexing. Yet surely they have their place in the inscrutable economy of the Universe.

You've done what you can. So relax, and—*with a shrug of resignation*—accept the fate of your object.

Qué será, será. What will be, will be.

3.
The Way
to Search

Betsy Finds Her Keys

Let's follow Betsy as she conducts a search—first the wrong way, then the right way!

•

Betsy reads Professor Solomon's HOW TO FIND LOST OBJECTS. She is intrigued by his method, and is sure that it will someday come in handy.

A few days later, she is about to leave for work, when . . . she can't find her keys.

"They must be in here," she mutters, and empties her brief-case on the floor.

Nope.

She looks everywhere.

Hmm, not in here.

Nor under here.

Where *are* they? she wonders.

Has the fish got them?

"Urghh!"

She's going nuts.

It's Professor Solomon, taking a stroll.

"Of course," says Betsy. "I forgot all about his method. The Twelve Principles! My keys aren't lost, *I* am."

She begins by applying the 3 C's.

Then it's Tail Thyself.

Betsy closes in on those elusive keys.

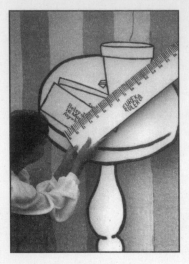

Determining her Eureka Zone.

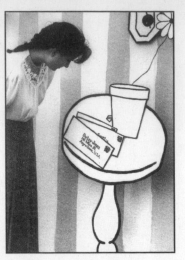

Exploring it.

Eureka!

She's mighty pleased.

And it's off to work.

"Next time," says Betsy, "I'll try the Twelve Principles *first.*"

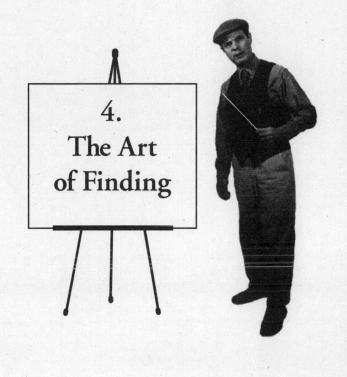

4.
The Art
of Finding

At My Door

People show up at my door, tell me they've lost this or that vital possession, and plead with me to help them find it.

I ask them: "What was the first thing you did when you realized it was missing?"

They shrug and reply: "I looked around the house for it."

"I thought so," I say, shaking my head sadly. "Well, you committed the Basic Blunder. Never 'look around' for a lost object."

That throws them for a loop. They stare at me and mutter: "Don't look around for it?"

"You heard me."

"Then what am I supposed to do?"

"Follow me and I'll show you."

I take them into the yard, where I make myself comfortable in a lawn chair and light up a cigar.

"This is how," I say to them. "How I find lost objects."

"But you're just sitting there."

"Not at all. I'm hard at work."

"That's work?"

"Indeed it is. I'm trying to find your lost object."

"You are? But how?"

"By applying the Three C's: Comfort, Calmness, and Confidence. By the way, what size head do you have? We'll want to make you a thinking cap."

At this point, many grow dubious and leave. I never see them again. Others decide to stick around and learn my method.

If you've come this far in the book, you're obviously among the latter. You've mastered the Twelve Principles, and now you are ready for a comprehensive look at the art of finding.

The sections that follow will deal with a variety of lost-object situations. Study these sections. Become familiar with the ins and outs of finding. Get a practical sense of what it's all about.

Then, the next time you lose something, you

should be able to find it with ease. It will be as if a genie were at your command, magically locating your object. Yet no magic will be involved—just *a method.*

A method that works.

How to Proceed

How should you go about using my method? What specific steps should you take in order to recover your object? How exactly is a search to be conducted?

There's no one answer to that. Finding is an art; and every Finder develops a style—an approach—a modus operandi—of his own. Moreover, every misplacement is unique and must be solved in an ad hoc fashion. But basically, here's what I tell people:

Sit down, make yourself comfortable, take a deep breath or two . . . and *ponder*. Ask yourself: Where *is* that object? In what obvious place? Try to recall or figure out its whereabouts. And the most effective means of doing that? The Twelve Principles, of course. Simply go through them, one by one, and see where they lead you. (If you haven't yet memorized the Principles, get out my book and hold it open to each Principle—as you sip coffee, think, scratch your head, reread the Principle, stare off into space, sigh, rack your brains, etc.)

When a possible location pops into mind, go check it out. If it's a dud, return to your seat and continue as above.

Remember, your frame of mind during this process is critical. Anxiety, self-reproach, haste—a Finder will have nothing to do with such Defeat Factors.

Instead, he is cool and collected. He sits and ponders, like a poet lost in reverie. He listens—to memories, brainstorms, hunches. And he searches with confidence.

But most of all, he *applies the Principles.*

If you proceed as I have outlined, you should have no trouble in tracking down your object.

Ten Tips

1.

One of the most common recovery areas for lost objects is the automobile. Your object may simply be lying on the car seat, where you left it. Or it may have become wedged between cushions, or have fallen on the floor. If you were traveling in an automobile, check these places. (And remember, check thoroughly. A cursory examination can be disastrous—as will be explained in "Common Mistakes to Beware.")

2.

Instead of being where it's supposed to be, your object may be where *something else* is supposed to be. What happened was a mental lapse, in which one routine motion got substituted for another. For example, your scissors are normally kept in a jar on the kitchen counter; but mindlessly, you returned them to the tool drawer.

3.

What were you wearing when you last remember having the object? Think back, then go search the pockets of those clothes. And be meticulous—search *every* pocket. The one you skip could be the one you're after.

4.

Are you one of those people who like to sprawl on the sofa? And your wallet—which you carry in a pants pocket—is missing? Maybe it fell out on the sofa. Go look.

It should be noted that dropping things is not the same as misplacing them: no lapse of memory is involved. So if a set of keys has fallen from your pocket, or an earring from your ear, most of the Principles will not be relevant. One that will be, however, is "Tail Thyself." Simply follow your trail about the house, closely examining the floor, stairs, seat cushions, etc.

5.

To reduce the likelihood of a misplacement, and to facilitate any searches that become necessary, keep your home neat and orderly. Remember the maxim: A PLACE FOR EVERYTHING AND EVERYTHING IN ITS PLACE.

6.

If a loss is thought to have occurred outside the home, sit down and review your movements during the day. Then telephone around, to see whether the item has been found. If it's a wallet, a bag, or a briefcase that may have been left in a store, have them check near the cash register: while paying, you may have put it down, then left it behind. Or if you dropped something, a good Samaritan may have found it and left it with the cashier. In the case of institutions—schools, community centers, theaters—ask if they have a lost-and-found.

Should this phone search prove fruitless (or not be feasible), leave the house and return to the locations you visited during the day. At each of them retrace your steps—keeping a sharp eye out for the object.

But remember: neither of the above should be resorted to prematurely. First search your house—search *your own immediate surroundings*. For that's usually where a missing object is. *Don't* race back in a panic to the supermarket—only to discover your wallet tucked away in the wrong section of your purse.

7.

Objects do disappear—thanks to thieves, trade rats, leprechauns, and the like. However, such incidents are infrequent, and their slight possibility must not provide an excuse for abandoning the search. Be steadfast. That diamond ring has simply been mislaid and can be found—if you are persistent and methodical.

8.

Be sure you're not looking for a phantom possession: something you had planned to purchase but then never did. (Or something you acquired in a dream.)

9.

As you sit and ponder the whereabouts of a lost object, your state of mind should be like that of a daydreamer: relaxed and contemplative. But when you get up to go check a site, *shift gears*. Be alert, energetic, and thorough—you're a detective now.

10.

Where has this object been found before? To what location does it seem to gravitate? Where has it turned up again and again?

Routinely, objects are mislaid in the same place—the same obvious place. Keys are left in locks. Briefcases in cars. Eyeglasses atop heads.

Try looking there . . . *before* you ransack the house.

Common Mistakes
to Beware

I see the same mistakes being made, again and again, in connection with lost objects. Among them are:

The Panicky Presumption

Pity the poor soul who goes through wastebaskets or garbage bags—or even races to the town dump! —in search of something that's right where it's supposed to be.

The Rash Accusation

"Who's got my coffee mug?" (or stapler or newspaper or elephant) we demand, after only a superficial search. A rash accusation—in what will probably prove a case of mere misplacement.

The Maniacal Search

Our misplacement throws us into a frenzy; like a wild man we search the entire house. We stalk about, rifling through drawers, emptying boxes, turning things inside out—and *utterly neglecting* the Twelve Principles.

Maniacal searches are undignified and exhausting. Worse yet, they tend to fail: an agitated eye will pass right over its quarry.

Apply the Principles!

Mistaken Image of an Object

I once helped a friend search his bookshelves for a particular book. He had described it to me as a hardback. So that's what we looked for—at length and in vain. Finally, I grew suspicious of his description, and began to examine the paperbacks as well. And there it was, in plain sight. Our false image of the book had prevented us from finding it.

Wild Goose Chase Suspicion

We are about to search our house for an object. Yet we suspect that it's not in the house, and that we are embarking on a Wild Goose Chase.

So we search half-heartedly—causing us to overlook the object. Which *convinces* us that it's not in the house.

Initial Discouragement

We've misplaced some tiny item—a pill, say, or a screw—and it could be anywhere in the house. We consider not even attempting a search. "I'm not going to find it," we murmur. "That darn thing's gone forever."

No! Say instead: "It is here somewhere, and I shall succeed in finding it. Why? Because I've got the Twelve Principles. Principles that work."

The Quick Look

As we sit and ponder the whereabouts of an object, a number of possible sites come to mind. So we take a Quick Look—a mere glance—into those nearest at hand. The idea is to move on to more promising sites. These initial ones, we tell ourselves, can always be returned to for a closer inspection.

A harmless expedient? Not if it results in an overlooked object. For we may *misremember* those initial sites as having been closely inspected, and never return to them.

NOTE: The Quick Look is not to be confused with the Cool Once-over. The Cool Once-over is a legitimate shortcut, and should precede any meticulous search. It works like this:

You suspect an object to be somewhere in a particular room, and are about to search that room. Before doing so, give it a general survey—an alert roving of the eye—a Cool Once-over. Your object may be sitting in plain sight. If so, you will spot it and avoid a meticulous search. If not, move *immediately* into the search. (Don't go off and survey other rooms, lest you fail to return to this one—a Quick Look after all!)

Quick Look

Cool Once-over

The Bermuda Triangle Myth

Can our possessions drop off the face of the earth? Is there a mysterious region into which they vanish, never to be seen again? Do supernatural forces or beings cause the disappearance of some objects?

Of course not (though an *occasional* leprechaun may pilfer things from the kitchen at night). Rather, one of the following phenomena may be involved:

Pocket Gobble

Absent-mindedly, we slip something into one of our pockets.

It's still there.

The Treasure-Trove Syndrome

We hide some valuables in a distinctive place—a location so unique that it will be sure to stick in our memory.

Oh yeah?

They're still there.

Ring-O-Ruption

We are making a household repair, when the telephone rings. Rushing to answer it, we drop the tool we were using on the first surface that presents itself.

It's still there.

The Hands Full Situation

Returning home with groceries, dry cleaning, and briefcase, we find our hands full. So in order to unlock the door, we set down one of those items. "Just for a second."

It's still there.

Be Right Back

A variation of the above. Rather than set something down, we struggle to unlock the door—then leave the keys in the lock, intending to return immediately and fetch them.

They're still there.

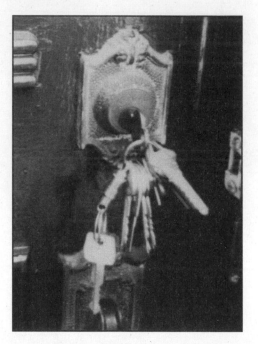

Loan-O-Loss

We loan something to a friend, then forget that we did so.

She's still got it.

•

The mind wants to believe that things mysteriously disappear—that they are spirited away by supernatural forces or beings. But (except for that pilfering leprechaun), it just isn't so. Most lost objects are *somewhere near at hand* . . . waiting to be found.

Your task is to find them.

The Sly Approach

You might want to try *outwitting* your object. As you sit and ponder, mutter that you haven't a clue as to its whereabouts. Or pretend not to care much about finding it. The idea is to lull the object into a false sense of security.

Then saunter over to where you suspect it to be—and pounce on it!

Step 1

Step 2

How to Make a
Thinking Cap

A thinking cap can boost your confidence, and focus
your mental energies. Here's how to make one.

1. Take a folded sheet
of newspaper and
locate its centerline.
Fold the upper cor-
ners down to meet
the centerline.

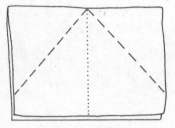

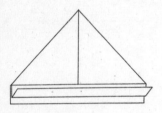

2. Fold the top sheet up
to meet the base of
the triangle.

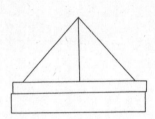

3. Fold it up again to
create the band of
the cap.

4. Turn the cap over and
fold the right and left
edges so that they
meet at the centerline.
(For a large-size cap,
let them fall an inch
short of the center-
line.)

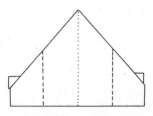

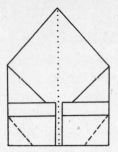

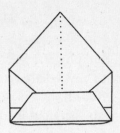

5. Fold the lower corners to
   the bottom of the band.

6. Fold the flap up over
   the band.

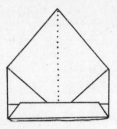

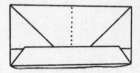

7. Fold the top of the flap
   down into the band.

8. Fold the peak of the
   cap down to the bottom
   of the band. Tuck it in.

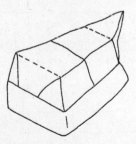

9. Open the cap and flatten
   its top. Fold the pointed
   ends down into the band.

10. Don the cap . . . and
    you're ready to *think*.

Eureka!

In Principle Ten we learned about the Eureka Zone —that limited area in which displaced objects tend to be found. It was described as a circle whose center is the original location of the object, and whose radius is eighteen inches.

There's a convenient way to determine your Eureka Zone; and that's by using a Eureka-Stik. They're easy to make—all you need is an ordinary ruler, the attachment on the next page, scissors, and tape. Start by cutting out the attachment. Then:

1. Fold along dotted line.
2. Fold tab A over tab B.
3. Tape them together.
4. Slide attachment onto end of ruler.
5. Tape it there.

And lo, a Eureka-Stik. Align its zero mark with the spot from which the object is suspected of having been displaced. Now rotate the arrow (see Figure 1). The circle described is your Eureka Zone.

Inspect every inch of that Zone—every nook and cranny. Check under and behind things. And don't

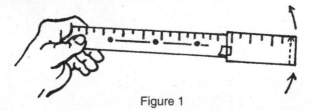

Figure 1

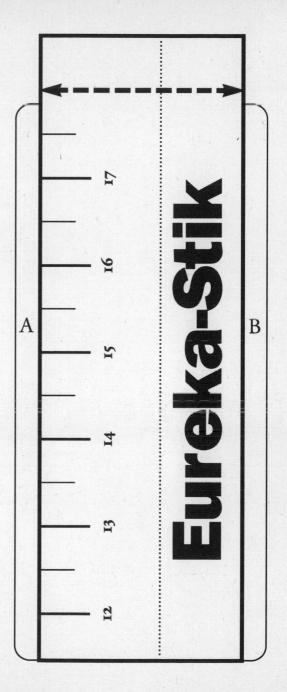

be fooled by vertical displacement—check the floor, too. (See note.)

Remember, your Eureka-Stik can be helpful, but it's not a magic wand. *How* you go about searching is what will make the difference.

NOTE: That eighteen inches assumes a simple case of horizontal displacement. But a vertical displacement may be involved as well (for example, a golf ball rolling off a desk and dropping to the floor), followed by a secondary horizontal displacement (the ball bouncing off somewhere). In such cases, use the formula

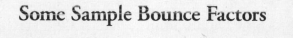

$$EZ = 18 + d + bf$$

where *EZ* is the Eureka Zone, *d* is the distance the object drops, and *bf* is the bounce factor. (Bounce factors range from 250 to zero. See table below.)

Also, in cases of oversized objects (brooms, ladders, surfboards, etc.), use a search radius of eighteen *feet*. And for missing files, check five folders in either direction.

Some Sample Bounce Factors

Object	bf (in inches)
Rubber ball	250
Lemon	10
Glass heirloom	0

The Purloined Letter

Hidden objects resemble misplaced ones in many respects, and may be searched for in a like manner. The classic tale of such a search is "The Purloined Letter" by Edgar Allan Poe. It goes as follows:

The Paris police are trying to recover a compromising letter that has been stolen from a royal personage. Believing it to be concealed in the home of a certain government official, they undertake a search of the premises.

Their search is meticulous. Every square inch of the apartment is scrutinized, every conceivable hiding place is looked into. Drawers are emptied—chairs are dismantled—cushions are probed with long needles. The floors, walls, and ceilings are examined with a microscope for signs of replastering. Yet the letter cannot be found.

C. Auguste Dupin, an aristocratic sleuth, is brought into the case. Using his powers of analysis, he conducts a search of his own . . . and locates the letter almost immediately.

When he delivers it to the police, they are amazed. Where was it? they want to know. How could their minute examination of the apartment have failed to uncover it?

Dupin smiles languidly, and explains that the official—aware that a meticulous search would be conducted for the letter—"had resorted to the comprehensive and sagacious expedient of not attempting to conceal it at all." Instead, the man had left it *in plain sight,* crumpled up as if unimportant and thrust carelessly into a rack.

And there the police ignored it. After all, the letter they were seeking would have been carefully preserved and tucked away in some secret place.

Had Dupin been familiar with the Twelve Principles, he might have told the red-faced gendarmes: "Messieurs, you were looking right at it."

The Game's Afoot

In "The Man with the Twisted Lip," Sherlock Holmes is engaged to locate a husband who has mysteriously disappeared. Watson gives this description of Holmes solving the case:

A large and comfortable double-bedded room had been placed at our disposal, and I was quickly between the sheets, for I was weary after my night of adventure. Sherlock Holmes was a man, however, who, when he had an unsolved problem upon his mind, would go for days, and even for a week, without rest, turning it over, rearranging his facts, looking at it from every point of view until he had either fathomed it or convinced himself that his data were insufficient. It was soon evident to me that he was now preparing for an all-night sitting. He took off his coat and waist-coat, put on a large blue dressing-gown, and then wandered about the room collecting pillows from his bed and cushions from the sofa and armchairs. With these he constructed a sort of Eastern divan, upon which he perched himself cross-legged, with an ounce of shag tobacco and a box of matches laid out in front of him. In the dim light of the lamp, I saw him sitting there, an old briar pipe between his lips, his eyes fixed vacantly upon the ceiling, the blue smoke curling up from him, silent, motionless, with the light shining upon his strong-set aquiline features. So he sat as I dropped off to sleep, and so he sat when a sudden ejaculation caused me to wake up, and I found the summer sun shining into the apartment. The pipe was still between his lips, the smoke still curling upward, and the room was full of a dense tobacco haze, but nothing remained of the heap of shag which I had seen upon the previous night.

"Awake, Watson?" he asked.

"Yes."

"Game for a morning drive?"

"Certainly."

"Then dress . . . " He chuckled to himself as he spoke, his eyes twinkled, and he seemed a different man to the somber thinker of the previous night.

What better example of someone applying the Three C's—Comfort, Calmness, and Confidence—as he begins a hunt!

Freud's Fee

According to Freud, objects may be intentionally misplaced. We *want* to forget where we left them. We *want* to overlook them.

In *The Psychopathology of Everyday Life*, he describes "the unconscious dexterity with which an object is mislaid on account of hidden but powerful motives." These motives involve "the low estimation in which the lost object is held, or a secret antipathy towards it or towards the person that it came from."

Freud tells of a patient who could not find the keys to his desk, despite a painstaking search of his apartment. Sensing that the loss was intentional—a "symptomatic act"—the patient had his servant take up the search. The servant found the keys.

The patient then delved into his unconscious. Why, he wondered, had he been unable to locate the keys? What had been his secret motive? Could it relate somehow to his treatment session with Freud, scheduled for the following day?

Suddenly, it dawned on him. Their loss had prevented a certain drawer from being opened—the drawer in which the money for his treatment was kept. His motive for losing the keys? Secret rage, he realized, at having to pay Freud so high a fee!

If you suspect your own misplacement to be intentional, have a friend join in the search.

Hrönir

In his story "Tlön, Uqbar, Orbis Tertius," Jorge Luis Borges tells of a world where (among other marvels) lost objects duplicate themselves. Thus, a searcher may come upon the object itself—or may have found its duplicate. Known as *hrönir*, these duplicates are usually mistaken for the object. They are not, however, exact copies. A *hrön* may be slightly larger than the original, and will possess some imperfection of form.

There are also *hrönir* that barely resemble the object that engendered them. Instead, they fulfill the searcher's desires in regard to that object. For example, he loses a pencil . . . and finds a fountain pen.

In the real world, *hrönir* shouldn't be a problem. But do take care to search for the actual object—not (as in my search for the supposedly hardcover book) an idealized image of it.

A True Account

The following letter is from Larry Callahan, an artist in Southern California, whom I had introduced to the Twelve Principles:

Dear Professor Solomon,

I had an experience recently that involved your method.

A friend needed a rental car; and I agreed to drive him to the airport to pick one up. I had some errands to run—letters to mail at the post office, and checks to deposit at my bank—so I decided to do it all in a single trip. I placed the letters and checks together in one pile (aware that this was reckless, but trusting myself to separate them at the appropriate moment), grabbed my car keys, and set out.

My first stop was the post office, where I deposited the letters in a curbside mailbox. Then I picked up my friend and proceeded to the airport.

At the rental agency he went inside, while I waited to make sure there was no problem. As I sat in my car, I noticed an accumulation of trash on the floor. Why not put these idle minutes to use, I said to myself, and do some car cleaning? So I gathered up the trash—bags, fliers, newspapers, and what-not—and dropped it into a receptacle outside the agency.

My friend emerged with a set of keys and a rental contract. I said goodbye and drove off, headed now for my bank.

At the bank I parked and looked about for those checks. They were nowhere to be seen. Frowning, I checked my pockets. I peered into the glove compartment. I poked about on the floor and under the seat. All to no avail. The checks had disappeared.

I tried not to panic. My anxiety level was rising, though—when I recalled your method. The Twelve Principles, I murmured. Why not give them a try?

The first that came to mind was "Don't look for it." Too late there—I had already searched the car. I moved on to "The three C's"—adjusting the seat to get comfortable, taking deep breaths to calm myself, and telling myself that the checks had to be SOME-WHERE.

Next came "You're looking right at it." I was? The checks were right in front of me? I glared at an empty dashboard.

Then I remembered the Principle about thinking back. So I thought back, trying to picture what I had done with the checks. AND I SAW MYSELF PUTTING THEM TOGETHER WITH THE LETTERS!

I groaned. It was obvious what had happened. I had dropped the whole pile into the mailbox—just as I had known I was capable of doing. What a ridiculous thing to have done! My checks were gone, swallowed up by the postal system.

But wait—maybe they were retrievable. A leviathan had swallowed them; but maybe I could descend into its belly and get them back. It was worth a try. Our local post office is a small, friendly place. Conceivably, they would take pity on me.

Trying to stay calm, I returned to the post office and explained to a postal employee what had happened. Other employees gathered to listen, and to shake their heads at my blunder. Was there any way to get the checks back? I asked. I was told that a procedure did exist for retrieving mail. I would have to fill out a form, and pay a small charge, for each item returned to me.

"Let's go for it," I said, trying to sound jocular.

First we looked through the hampers in the back room.

87

Plenty of mail, but no loose checks. Then we went outside, opened the mailboxes, and checked their contents. Still no checks.

I racked my brains. Where else could they be? Think back.

I thought back . . . and saw myself gathering up that trash in my car.

O no. The checks must have fallen on the floor, and been in with the trash.

"That's it!" I cried. "They're in the trash can!"

I described this new theory to the postal employees. They began to look at me funny. Bidding them a hasty farewell, I dashed to my car and drove back to the airport.

At the rental agency I got out of my car and eyed the trash receptacle. I removed its lid and looked in. There was nothing inside. The receptacle had been emptied since my departure.

By the garage were a pair of rubbish bins. I approached them, hoisted myself up on one of them, and peered inside—at a mass of rubbish. In these bins the agency emptied its trash; and in these bins, I was convinced, were my checks. O my, what was I to do?

I could do the sensible thing and admit defeat. After all, the checks were replaceable. It would be tiresome and embarrassing; but I could contact each client, explain my blunder, and ask for a new check.

Or—the indignity be damned!—I could search through the bins.

I decided to search.

Taking a deep breath, I climbed into the bin and sank knee-deep in trash. The agency disposed of a large quantity of computer printouts; and had it not been for the coffee grounds, pencil shavings, and snack remains mixed in, I might have enjoyed as a lark my descent into this binful of paper. But I persevered.

Finding nothing in the first bin, I hopped out and climbed into the second.

Incredibly, after a bit of digging, I found my checks. They were among some contract forms and crushed cups. I emerged from that bin knowing more than I cared to about the underbelly of the car-rental business. But I had my checks.

Without the Principles I would never have found them. Your method is invaluable, for people like me when we do something stupid! Much thanks.

Yours,
Larry

The above is a testimonial, which I appreciate. But it is also a cautionary tale. For the truth is that *Larry was lucky*. Let's take a look at his case.

Yes, he emerged from the rubbish bin triumphantly clutching his checks. They were in there. But they could just as easily have been under his car seat, between the cushions, in the glove compartment, or in one of his pockets. While he may have looked in these places, he does not seem to have looked well. "I checked . . . I peered . . . I poked about," he tells us—describing a search that sounds to me cursory and incomplete.

In other words, he should have begun with a *meticulous* search of his car. Instead, he took a Quick Look, then succumbed to one Panicky Presumption after another. They're in the mailbox! he cried —no, the trash can!—no, the bin! That one of these long shots happened to pan out does not justify his failure to have eliminated first the more likely sites.

Descending into a rubbish bin must always remain a last resort.

5.
This and
That

Some Quotes

There is no such thing as a lost movie—only mislaid movies. And I shall find them.

—MILES KREUGER, FILM HISTORIAN

•

Last Saturday morning, I concluded that there is nothing harder to find than a bottle of pancake syrup reshelved six inches away from its accustomed spot.

—BURTON HILLIS, COLUMNIST FOR BETTER HOMES AND GARDENS

•

Having nothing, nothing can he lose.

—SHAKESPEARE

•

When does a poor man rejoice? When he loses something and finds it again.

—YIDDISH PROVERB

•

The quickest way to find something you've lost or misplaced is to purchase another just like it.

—GEORGE BERGMAN

Missing Luggage

If an airline, railway, or bus line has lost your luggage, you and they can work together to find it.

For example, I once took a train to Charlottesville, Virginia. To my dismay, my checked baggage failed to arrive with me. The clerk at Amtrak attempted to track it down but several days went by and still no baggage. Finally, I happened to look closely at my claim check, and saw that it read *Charlotte*. I pointed this out to the clerk, who contacted the station in Charlotte, North Carolina. And yes, my baggage was there.

Another time, I arrived in Santa Monica, California, by bus and the baggage clerk was unable to find a pair of boxes I had checked. My heart sank and I was resigning myself to never again seeing those boxes—when a mad hope gripped me. I asked if I might enter the baggage room and look about for them. The clerk allowed me to do so . . . and there were my boxes, sitting on a rack. Somehow he had overlooked them.

In each case I had feared the worst: the disappearance of my stuff into some black hole for luggage. Yet a cooperative effort led to recovery.

How Not to Lose Things

Some of us are prone to losing things. Friends laugh and say: "He'd lose his head if it weren't nailed on."

Maybe that's not such a bad idea.

To prevent pens from "walking away," banks chain them to the counter. And some men carry a wallet that is chained to their belts.

If your possessions tend to drift off, consider tying them down.

The man pictured below says he never loses anything.

The Last Place

I had the following conversation with a dentist, as he cleaned my teeth:

DENTIST: Do you know where a lost object always is?

PROF. SOLOMON: Where?

DENTIST: In the last place you look.

PROF. SOLOMON: You mean, the last place you'd think of looking?

DENTIST: No, the last place you look. Because as soon as you find it, you stop looking.

PROF. SOLOMON: That's pretty good. May I use it in my book?

DENTIST: Sure.

A Consumer's Guide to Detection Devices

Looking for a lost-object detection device? Consider the following:

The Findometer

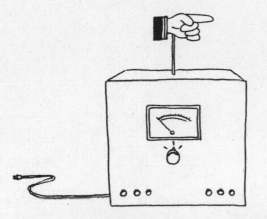

Larry Callahan (that artist who descended into a rubbish bin) has designed the above contraption. He claims that misplaced objects "disturb the energy flow" of a room—a phenomenon that his machine would be able to detect. The hand, he says, would rotate in the direction of the disturbance.

How would the Findometer work? By applying modern electronics to *feng shui*, the ancient Chinese art of geomancy.

Sounds good.

Key Beeper

Attached to your key ring, this device will beep repeatedly in response to a clap—thus revealing the location of your keys. Unfortunately, any clap will do; and a key beeper may go off unexpectedly.

Divining Rods

Well diggers, prospectors, treasure hunters, and other practitioners of "dowsing" swear by these. I find them unreliable. Still, they're lightweight and easy to use. Grip the horns firmly. Then just wander about until you feel a twitch.

Divining rods have been around for thousands of years. The Egyptians used them to foretell the future; the Romans located precious metals with them.

Traditionally, they are fashioned from the branch of a hazel tree. A plastic version may be found in novelty shops.

The MOC

If you've dropped a small object containing iron, you might want to try a MOC, or Magnetic Object Collector. (It's basically just a magnet.) Drag it about the general area of your loss, until the MOC picks up your object.

Can be attached to the family dog.

Knee Pads and Miner's Lamp

These are for crawling about on your hands and knees, as you search for something.

But why are you crawling about? Go find a comfortable chair, and apply the Principles!

Alternative Methods

There are methods besides my own for finding a lost object (although none of them can rival the Twelve Principles for efficacy, reliability, and ease of application). You might want to try one of the following:

Hypnosis

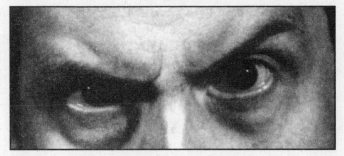

Should be administered by a qualified professional.

Memory Elixirs

Grandma's Principle

A friend in Ontario writes:

> When my grandmother wanted to find something
> that was lost, she would stop in the middle of the room
> and ask herself out loud, "Now if I were a (whatever
> was lost), where would I go?" She'd muse on that one,
> and proceed to wherever she decided the thing would
> have gone to—and there it was!

Hand Tremblers

Members of the Navaho tribe consult a Hand Trem-
bler. The quivering of his hands leads them to lost
objects.

Dreams

It is not unknown for the location of a missing
object to be revealed in a dream. So keep an eye out
even while asleep.

Storefront Psychics

They will employ their mystic powers to locate your object.

Saint Anthony

Our efforts to track down a lost object—by whatever method—are sometimes doomed to failure.

When that happens, it may be time to turn to a Higher Power.

Catholics have traditionally prayed to Saint Anthony for the restoration of lost objects. A promise is sometimes made that—in return for his services—a donation will be made to the poor. These donations are known as Saint Anthony's Bread.

Children chant the refrain:

> Saint Anthony, please, come around
> Something's been lost and can't be found.

Saint Anthony may also be called upon in cases of lost faith, hope, or love.

105

Hashevat Aveida

The Talmud contains a set of laws regarding *hashevat aveida*, or the return of lost objects. Essentially, a person is bound to return—or make a serious attempt to return—any lost object he has found. Nor may he accept a reward for this service.

There are, of course, exceptions and complications. The duty is waived if the object's owner can be expected to have given up hope for its return. And one must be sure the object was lost. If there are signs of its having been deliberately left where it was found, then the object must not be removed—since to do so would *cause* its loss.

But the basic idea is that finders are *not* keepers—in order that losers not be weepers.

This *mitzvah* (commandment, obligation, good deed) has led to the establishment in Jewish communities of special bulletin boards, on which people who have lost or found something may put up notices. One such bulletin board in Jerusalem is a city-block long!

A Zen *Koan*

A monk had misplaced his rice bowl—somewhere in a dark room. He was groping about the room in search of it, when the abbot of the monastery came in and asked what he was doing. The monk explained.

"Why don't you go outside and look for it?" said the abbot. "There's more light out there."

Wannamoho

I would like to conclude with a tale. It's about Lone Cloud, and how he learned that some lost objects should stay lost!

•

One day Lone Cloud got lost in the forest. On and on he walked, sure that he would soon come upon a path. But the forest grew denser, the shadows deeper. Now and again rose the cry of the raven—an eerie sound in this pathless place. And Lone Cloud began to feel anxious.

I'm truly lost, he thought.

Then the forest came to an end, and Lone Cloud found himself descending into a valley. Only grass grew in this valley. Winding its way through the grass was a stream.

As he walked along, Lone Cloud was surprised by what he saw scattered in the grass. For everywhere were articles of daily life—bows, arrows, traps, pots, bowls, balls, whistles, bracelets, cloaks, moccasins.

Lone Cloud noticed the raven, perched on a basket. "Where am I?" he asked the wisest of creatures.

"In Wannamoho," said the raven, "the Valley of Lost Things. Strewn about you are the missing possessions of your people."

"Our missing possessions?"

"Yes. They have been coming here for countless generations—ever since the first of your ancestors mislaid something."

"But how do they get here?"

"They are brought by the Wind That Laughs. The moment something is given up for lost, he laughs—and wafts it to this valley."

Lone Cloud—who had never heard of Wannamoho—gazed about in wonder. The Valley of Lost Things! And he recalled a pouch he had lost years before. Richly embroidered, it had contained a fine pipe and powerful tobacco. How precious that pouch had been to him, and how he would like it back!

"The pouch I mislaid—it is here in this valley?"

"It is."

"Show me where. I shall retrieve it and take it back with me."

"I wouldn't do that. Your pouch belongs now in Wannamoho. To remove it could bring bad luck upon you."

"Nonsense," said Lone Cloud. And he insisted the raven lead him to his pouch.

So the raven flew into the air, circled about, and

fluttered down to the grass. Lone Cloud came running over—and there was his lost pouch.

"Aha!" he cried, grabbing it up. He opened it and beheld his pipe and tobacco. Amazingly, the tobacco was still pungent.

Pleased to have regained his pouch, Lone Cloud departed from the valley and wandered the forest. At last he came upon a path, and by dusk was back at his hut.

That night he filled the pipe and smoked it. And he was puffing away and murmuring pleasurably and thinking that this indeed was how to spend his evenings (and maybe his days, too)—when his hut collapsed about him!

Dazed, Lone Cloud crawled out of the ruins. And he wondered: Could this be that bad luck of which the raven had warned?

The next day Lone Cloud was gathering nuts—when the ground opened and he plunged into a bear trap! Bruised and abashed, he climbed out. More bad luck?

And the next day he woke up itching. A rash covered his body—poison ivy.

"It is as the raven said," lamented Lone Cloud. "He warned me that reclaiming my pouch might bring bad luck. And so it has."

Lone Cloud searched until he found the raven, perched in an oak. "You were right," he said. "I have brought bad luck upon myself. Tell me what I must do to get rid of it."

"The pouch must go back to Wannamoho," said the raven. "Only then will this bad luck leave you."

So Lone Cloud roamed the forest, looking for the Valley of Lost Things. He wanted to return the pouch to where he had found it. But try as he might, he could not locate that strange valley.

"What am I to do?" he groaned. "Until this pouch is back in Wannamoho, misfortune will hound me."

Returning to the ruins of his hut, he found the raven perched there. "Wisest of creatures," said Lone Cloud, "I looked and looked, but could not find Wannamoho."

"It is hard to find."

"How then am I to return this pouch? Perhaps you could take it back for me?" said Lone Cloud, holding out the pouch.

"O no," said the raven.

"Then what am I to do?"

"Go help the beaver."

Strange advice, thought Lone Cloud. But he walked along the river until he found the beaver, who was

dragging a tree into the water. "Let me help you," he said to the most industrious of creatures.

"I could use some help," said the beaver. "Come, lend me a hand."

So Lone Cloud put down his pouch and joined the beaver. All day they labored together—felling trees, dragging them to the river, and building a dam. The work was strenuous, and Lone Cloud wanted to quit. But he was determined to do as the raven had advised.

Finally, the beaver thanked him and swam off. Lone Cloud sighed with relief. He was tired and hungry; it was time to go home and eat. He looked about for his pouch.

But where was it? He had left it by the river—but where exactly he couldn't recall.

"Where's that pouch?" cried Lone Cloud.

Up and down the river he searched for it. He seemed to remember having left it under a bush—but which bush? For a long time he searched, but without success.

Finally he gave up, plopped to the ground, and sat there frowning. A wind rustled in the trees.

But then his frown dissolved, and a gleam entered his eye. For he realized he had lost the pouch again.

And that meant it was back in Wannamoho.

Lone Cloud jumped for joy, glad to be free of the ill luck that had plagued him.

A Final Word

I hope this book has taught you how to locate what you lose.

If it has, enter your name on the certificate. You are now a Finder, not a Loser. You are a master of the right way—the *effective* way—to search for lost objects.

And please write to me. I want to hear any stories, inspirational or otherwise, of how the Twelve Principles have worked for you.

Remember, lost objects *can* be found. They *want* to be found. And they *will* be found—by SYSTEMATIC SEARCHERS.

Searchers for whom finding things is not a chore, but a challenge.

Searchers who—instead of ransacking their own house—sit down, don their thinking cap, take a sip of tea, half-close their eyes, and murmur:

"All right, the game's afoot!"

Searchers like yourself.

Certificate of Proficiency

This is to Certify that

_____

has mastered the TWELVE PRINCIPLES,
and is qualified to search for Lost Objects.

Prof. Solomon
_____

Index